Bows,

Bullets,

and Bears

True Stories about
Settlers, Soldiers, Indians, and Outlaws
on the Pennsylvania Frontier

JOHN L. MOORE

Mechanicsburg, Pennsylvania   USA

Published by Sunbury Press, Inc.
50 West Main Street, Suite A
Mechanicsburg, Pennsylvania 17055

www.sunburypress.com

Although the people whose experiences are chronicled in this book are dead, their stories survive in letters, diaries, journals, official reports, depositions, interrogations, examinations, minutes, and memoirs. These sources are quoted liberally. An occasional ellipsis indicates where words or phrases have been omitted. Punctuation and spelling have been modernized.

Copyright © 2013 by John L. Moore.
Cover copyright © 2014 by Sunbury Press.

Sunbury Press supports copyright. Copyright fuels creativity, encourages diverse voices, promotes free speech, and creates a vibrant culture. Thank you for buying an authorized edition of this book and for complying with copyright laws by not reproducing, scanning, or distributing any part of it in any form without permission. You are supporting writers and allowing Sunbury Press to continue to publish books for every reader. For information contact Sunbury Press, Inc., Subsidiary Rights Dept., 50-A W. Main St., Mechanicsburg, PA 17011 USA or legal@sunburypress.com.

For information about special discounts for bulk purchases, please contact Sunbury Press Orders Dept. at (855) 338-8359 or orders@sunburypress.com.

To request one of our authors for speaking engagements or book signings, please contact Sunbury Press Publicity Dept. at publicity@sunburypress.com.

ISBN: 978-1-62006-511-2 (Trade Paperback)
Library of Congress Control Number: 2014956268

FIRST SUNBURY PRESS EDITION: October 2014

Product of the United States of America
0 1 1 2 3 5 8 13 21 34 55

Set in Bookman Old Style
Designed by Lawrence Knorr
Cover by Lawrence Knorr
Cover Art "She Claims the Rock Shelter" by Andrew Knez, Jr.
Edited by Janice Rhayem

Continue the Enlightenment!

JOHN L. MOORE's

FRONTIER PENNSYLVANIA SERIES

Bows, Bullets, & Bears
Cannons, Cattle, & Campfires
Forts, Forests, & Flintlocks
Pioneers, Prisoners, & Peace Pipes
Rivers, Raiders, & Renegades
Settlers, Soldiers, & Scalps
Traders, Travelers, & Tomahawks
Warriors, Wampum, & Wolves

Dedication

For Robert B. Swift, with whom I have explored many
battlefields, graveyards, mountains, rivers, islands,
trails, roads, and libraries.

Acknowledgments

Jane P. Moore, Thomas J. Brucia, and Robert B. Swift read the manuscript and suggested a variety of improvements.

Murder in the Woods: Trader Disappears

February 1744

By the early 1740s, an Indian trader named Jack Armstrong, who operated out of Lancaster County, had developed a reputation for employing sharp and even antagonistic practices in his dealings with the Delaware Indians who lived, hunted, and trapped along the Susquehanna and the Juniata Rivers. Some of the trader's white friends had even cautioned him about being overly harsh with his Indian customers and especially about angering them. If Armstrong wasn't particularly likeable, he was nevertheless a successful trader and a well-known frontier personality. But as hard and tough as Armstrong was, events that occurred along the Juniata River during early 1744 proved that one of his customers, a Delaware Indian known as John Musemeelin, was tougher, harder, and more ferocious.

Armstrong's story begins in early 1744 when the trader and two men who worked for him, James Smith and Woodworth Arnold, loaded their string of pack horses with trade goods—gun powder, gun flints, lead bullets, glass beads, scissors, woolen blankets, combs, little bells, and other items. For such goods, native trappers would eagerly swap the skins of deer, bears, beavers, elk, otters, foxes, raccoons, and wildcats.

The three men headed north and followed the trail along the Susquehanna, and then, well north of present-day Harrisburg, swung west and headed out the Juniata toward the Allegheny Mountains. That was in February. By late March and early April, as spring came on, a rumor swept across the frontier: Armstrong and his men had disappeared and weren't ever coming out of the woods.

As it turned out, all three had been murdered. Since the killings took place in Indian Country—well beyond what was then the western boundary of Pennsylvania—an Indian chief conducted the first official inquiry in the case. Indeed, records of the Pennsylvania colony contain a detailed account of this chief's investigation into the disappearance and murder of Jack Armstrong. The account itself was dictated by Chief Shikellamy, an Oneida who represented the Iroquois Confederacy at Shamokin and who led the investigation that exposed the killer. Located at the forks of the Susquehanna River, Shamokin was the largest Indian town in what is now Pennsylvania. Shikellamy subsequently had the man arrested and incarcerated. Conrad Weiser, a Pennsylvania German who was the colony's Indian agent, recorded Shikellamy's narrative.

For more than half a century, the Pennsylvania frontier had been a reasonably peaceful place where white traders and other travelers had been free to come and go at will. Shikellamy's fast handling of the case may well have prevented a shooting war between Indians and whites living in the border regions.

Shikellamy, who functioned as a sort of territorial governor for the Six Nations in the Susquehanna River Valley, looked into Armstrong's disappearance. When he found ample evidence of murder and a cover-up, the chief ordered arrests and a trial. Weiser's report, which he submitted to Governor George Thomas, consisted of Shikellamy's findings and conclusions.

Nearly 270 years later, some facts remain murky, but others seem clear, and these help in uncovering essential details of the affair. To begin with, there's no disputing that Musemeelin, who lived in the region and was known in Shamokin, owed a debt to Jack Armstrong. Musemeelin was an experienced hunter and trapper. At some time prior to January 1744, the two men did some trading: Armstrong gave goods to

Portrait of Oneida chief Swatane (a.k.a. Shikellamy) by Jacques Reich (probably based on an earlier work by another artist) Appletons' Cyclopædia of American Biography, v. 6, 1889, p. 5

Musemeelin in exchange for furs that Musemeelin had caught. The two had apparently done business previously, because the trader extended credit to the trapper, and the records say that the deal ended with Musemeelin owing "some furs" to Armstrong. That transaction took place well beyond the boundaries of the Pennsylvania Colony, so there wasn't much in the way of enforcement of any colonial laws that might have regulated it.

When Armstrong arbitrarily decided that Musemeelin was taking too much time to satisfy the debt, the trader demanded the Indian's horse and flintlock rifle as collateral. Musemeelin wasn't at all happy about this, but Armstrong seized the horse and ordered James Smith, who worked for him, to take Musemeelin's gun, which Smith did.

Indians living along the Susquehanna frequently hunted along the Juniata, and Musemeelin had a hunting cabin along a well-used forest thoroughfare known as the Juniata Path, which had its eastern terminus on the Susquehanna at present-day Dalmatia.

One day during the winter, Armstrong met Musemeelin along the Juniata trail, and the Indian paid all but twenty shillings of the debt. He offered to pawn a neck-belt he was wearing, but the trader refused to do this. Musemeelin argued that since he had paid off much of the debt, Armstrong should at least return his horse. But the trader refused and countered that Musemeelin had taken so long to make payments that he now owed a great deal of interest. According to the records, this was Jack Armstrong's "usual custom," and it enraged Musemeelin. The two quarreled, and the records state "the Indian went away in great anger without his horse to his hunting cabin."

The Missing Men

In the weeks after this, Armstrong's brothers, James and Alexander, became concerned when the trader and his men failed to return home. Their fears grew when they heard rumors that some Indians had murdered them. In late March, with the trader still missing, his brothers and a number of their friends met at the home of Joseph Chambers, who lived along the Susquehanna north of present-day Harrisburg and immediately south of the Blue Mountain. They decided to travel up the river and visit Sassoonan, the Delaware king at Shamokin who was also known as Allumapees, and to confer with Shikellamy as well.

Most of the people living at Shamokin were Delaware Indians, but there were also Iroquois and Tutelo Indians in residence. Allumapees was the headman of the Delawares. Shikellamy, as the Iroquois half king, had broad oversight over all the native peoples living along the Susquehanna and its tributaries, which included the Juniata.

By the time the Armstrong brothers arrived, Shikellamy may have already overheard rumors about the murders. Indeed, a young Delaware known as both Jimmy and Billy had come to Shamokin soon after he and another young Delaware had been hunting along the Juniata with Musemeelin. As Shikellamy later told Conrad Weiser, after Jimmy left town, "it was whispered about that some of the Delaware Indians had killed Armstrong and his men."

More specifically, Shikellamy said, "A drunken Indian came to one of the Tutelos houses at night and told the man of the house that he could tell him a piece of bad news. 'What is that?' said the other. The drunken man said, 'Some of our Delaware Indians have killed Armstrong and his men.'"

At Shamokin, the Armstrongs and their friends visited with both Allumapees and Shikellamy and told both that they intended to ride over to the Juniata and search for their missing brother. The chiefs agreed that a number of Indians from Shamokin should accompany them, and they ordered eight men to go with the Armstrongs and their friends to the house of James Berry, who lived about twenty miles south of

Shamokin. In the morning they would all leave for the Juniata from Berry's house.

The vigilantes and Indians left Shamokin and made their way to Berry's place without incident, but during the night, three of the Indians ran off. In the morning the Armstrongs, "together with ye five Indians that remained, set on their journey peaceably to the last supposed sleeping place of the deceased," the brothers said later in a deposition. They had traveled along the Juniata to the vicinity of present-day Mount Union. Satisfied that they had probably found Armstrong's camp, the nine members of the posse spread out and began a close search of the ground. They hadn't gone very far when Berry "came to a white oak tree which had three notches on it, and close by said tree he found a shoulder bone."

The frontiersman picked up the bone and examined it closely then took it to the camp and showed it to his friends. They concluded that it probably was Armstrong's. For reasons not specified, they also agreed that after Armstrong had been killed, he had been "eating (sic) by the Indians ..." (Why did they think this? Were there cut marks such as those made by a knife on the bone?) The deposition that white members of the posse made on April 19, 1744, is silent on this point. It does say, however, that they suspected one of the five Indians in their party had taken part in the killing. According to the document, when one of the white men handed the shoulder bone to this man, "as soon as the said Indian took the bone in his hand, his nose gushed out with blood, and he directly handed it to another."

After this incident, the searchers traveled along the Juniata for another three or four miles when, just west of present-day Mount Union, they reached a pass where the river courses through a long ridge now known as Jacks Mountain. They all crossed over to an island and stopped to discuss what to do next.

They were close to the spot where the Frankstown Path, a major east-west trail between the

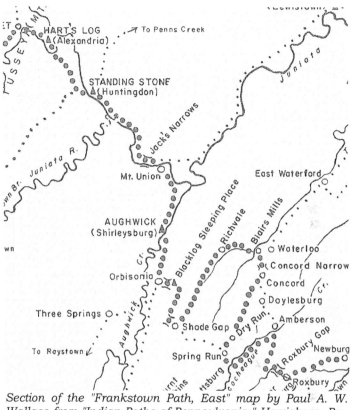

*Section of the "Frankstown Path, East" map by Paul A. W.
Wallace from "Indian Paths of Pennsylvania." Harrisburg: Pa.,
Historical and Museum Commission, 1971.*

Susquehanna and Allegheny rivers, crossed the
Juniata. At some point the white men decided that
they would follow one side of the river, and they
directed the Indians to cross over and proceed along
the other side. The whites left the island and, moving
slowly, began to study the ground for clues or signs.
They soon realized that although one of the Delawares
had crossed to the far bank, the other four were
following them "at a small distance" on the same side
of the river.

Suddenly one of the whites looked up and saw "some bald eagles and other fowls" circling above the river. The men lost sight of the Indians as they hurried downriver, where they spotted a corpse, which they quickly identified as the body of James Smith, one of Jack Armstrong's men. As they said later, "directly upon finding the corpse, these deponents heard three shots of guns, which they had great reason to think was the Indians, their companions, who had deserted from them." To signal the Indians that they had found the body, the men fired three gunshots, "but to no purpose, for they never saw the Indians anymore."

They continued their search. "About (a) quarter of a mile farther down ... they saw more bald eagles, whereupon they made down towards the place, where they found another corpse ... lying on a rock." It was the body of Armstrong's other man, Woodworth Arnold.

After that they returned to Armstrong's camp, where they had arranged to meet the Indians. They saw that "the Indians had been there and cooked some victuals for themselves and had gone off." The Delawares never returned. The whites spent the night at the spot, but their sleep was repeatedly interrupted by the barking of one man's dog. The animal hadn't barked previously during the trip. This fact troubled the men and gave them "great reason to suspect that the Indians was (sic) then thereabout and intended to do them some damages." Rather than try to continue sleeping, they stood behind trees and kept watch with their guns cocked, but the rest of the night passed without incident.

In the morning the men returned to the stretch of river where they had found the bodies of Smith and Arnold. As they prepared to bury them, they had ample time to examine their wounds. There were "ghastly and deep cuts on their heads," clearly made with "a tomahawk or such like weapon, which had sunk into their skulls and brains." Near the gash on

8

JACK'S NARROWS, NEAR MAPLETON, ON THE PENNSYLVANIA RAILROAD.

A mid-9th century engraving of Jack's Narrows and Jack's Mountain along the Pennsylvania Railroad.

one man's skull, "there appears a hole" that they "believe to be a bullet hole."

The men buried the bodies "as decently as their circumstances would allow" then decided to return to the Paxton settlements along the Susquehanna. When they didn't encounter any of the Delawares who had accompanied them, they decided against traveling the Juniata Path, which was probably the way they had come from Shamokin a few days earlier. Instead, they took "the Allegheny Road to John Harris's, thinking it dangerous to return the same way they went out."

The Allegheny Road, also known as the Frankstown Path, dropped well to the south of the Juniata trail, which left the Juniata at present-day Thompsontown and swung northeast to McKee's Half Falls and modern Dalmatia, where it ended.

Anxiety in Shamokin

As March yielded to April, the exact sequence of events in the Armstrong case becomes difficult to track. When the Armstrong brothers and their friends followed the trail back to Paxton, they approached likely spots for ambush slowly and warily. In Shamokin, meanwhile, the Delawares and Iroquois grew increasingly anxious, especially as the Indians who had helped look for the traders returned to town and reported that all three bodies had been found. As the news spread through Shamokin, Allumapees, who was well- and widely known for his alcoholism, got—and stayed—drunk.

At some point one of the drunken Delawares confided to his Tutelo neighbors that he feared the murders might well create "a disturbance between us and the white people" who lived in the region. The whites would be enraged if the killers went unpunished. To keep the peace with the whites, "I will kill them myself," the Delaware declared.

At this juncture, Conrad Weiser enters the story. He and Shikellamy had developed a strong friendship and working relationship over the years, and the morning that Shikellamy heard the rumor about the murders, "Shikellamy and some other Indians of the Delawares were called to assist Allumapees in council," Weiser reported. In turn, the Delaware council advised the chief to call upon a Delaware medicine man to help him expose the murderers. Shikellamy later told Weiser that the shaman "was busy all night" with his conjuring. The next morning he directed Allumapees to question two young Delawares—John, son of Neshaleeny, and Jemmy, or Jimmy, who was also called Billy. "They were present when Armstrong was killed," the shaman advised.

Accompanied by two other Delawares, Allumapees first went to interrogate Jimmy/Billy. "He told the whole story very freely," Shikellamy said later. "Then they went to the other, but he would not say a word ..."

Allumapees and his companions listened closely as Jimmy described the events in which he had participated on the Juniata, but nobody took any notes. During subsequent weeks and months, the young man told and retold his story many times. Eventually, Jimmy's lengthy and highly detailed version made its way into Pennsylvania's colonial records as a key part of Shikellamy's official narrative of his investigation. As the colony's Indian agent, Weiser incorporated Shikellamy's statement in the May 2, 1744, report that he submitted to the governor. Here is Jimmy's statement as Shikellamy retold it and as Weiser wrote it down. (Passages enclosed in quotation marks are taken directly from Weiser's report.)

Hunting for Bears

Several weeks after Musemeelin and Armstrong quarreled about the Indian's horse, the trader and the two men who worked for him, Smith and Arnold, passed Musemeelin's Juniata cabin as they headed to the Ohio River. They had a string of pack horses loaded with bundles of trade goods and furs. Musemeelin wasn't at home, but his wife was, and she demanded that Armstrong return the horse. Armstrong said he couldn't do this because he "had by this time sold or lent the horse to James Berry." Berry lived about twenty miles south of Shamokin and about forty miles north of Harris's Ferry.

When Musemeelin returned from hunting, "his wife told him that Armstrong was gone by, and ... pressed him to pursue and take revenge of Armstrong."

Jimmy and John, son of Neshaleeny, often went hunting with Musemeelin. Three days after Armstrong had passed by, Musemeelin said to them, "Come, let us go towards the Great Hills to hunt bears." The Great Hills were a reference to the Allegheny Mountains in western Pennsylvania.

Armed with flintlock hunting rifles, the three Indians carried their bullets in leather pouches and stored their gunpowder in powder horns. They also carried hunting knives and tomahawks. For native hunters, all this was standard equipment.

Musemeelin led the way, and "after they had gone a good way, Musemeelin … was told by the two young men that they were out of their course. 'Come you along,' said Musemeelin, and they accordingly followed him till they came to the path that leads to the Ohio. Then Musemeelin told them he had a good mind to go and fetch his horse back from Armstrong, and desired the two young men to come along. Accordingly they went. It was then almost night, and they travelled till next morning."

At some point after daybreak, Musemeelin told Jimmy and John that he thought they were getting close to Armstrong and his men. He stopped walking and took a container of black war paint from a leather pouch around his neck. As he applied the paint to his face, Musemeelin told Jimmy and John to also blacken their faces. He explained that the white men would be frightened to see three Indians with blackened faces.

Musemeelin laughed when he said this, and "the young men thought he joked as he used to do," Shikellamy said. "They did not blacken themselves, but he did."

Delaware Indians often painted their faces black when they went on the warpath.

"When the sun was above the trees, or about an hour high," the Indians came to Armstrong's campfire.

"They found James Smith sitting, and they also sat down. Musemeelin asked where Jack was. Smith told him that he was gone to clear the road a little. Musemeelin said he wanted to speak with him, and went that way." As Musemeelin walked off, "he said something and looked back laughing." But Jimmy and John were talking with Smith and didn't hear what Musemeelin had said.

John and Jimmy told Smith that they were hungry. Since they were sitting along the bank of the Juniata, Smith told them to kill some game, which was plentiful, and they "would make some bread, and by and by they would all eat together." This was a reasonable suggestion, and just as the Indians were about get up, "they heard a gun go off not far off."

A little later, they learned that Musemeelin had just shot and killed Woodworth Arnold.

In a while, Musemeelin returned to the campsite, displeased to see that James Smith was still alive. "Why did you not kill that white man according as I bid you," he said. "I have laid the other two down."

Since Musemeelin was speaking in Delaware, Smith didn't understand a word, but Musemeelin's remark terrified Jimmy, who ran off toward the river.

With his back toward Musemeelin, Smith still sat by the fire, which was inside a ring of rocks. Nearby, an ax lay alongside a stack of firewood. Musemeelin grabbed the ax and hit Smith with it. He "struck it three times into Smith's head before he died. Smith never stirred. Then he told the young Indian to call the other; but he was so terrified he could not call. Musemeelin then went and fetched him, and said to him that two of the white men were killed."

Musemeelin said he was now going to find Jack Armstrong and kill him. He told Jimmy and John that they were going along and started to walk rapidly down the trail ahead of them.

The young Indians followed reluctantly, and John said: "My friend, don't you kill any of the white people. Let him do what he will. I have not killed Smith. He has done it himself. We have no need to do such a barbarous thing."

Musemeelin was a good distance ahead of the other Indians when he came upon Armstrong sitting upon an old log. Nearby was a camp fire.

Armstrong didn't show any fear even though he obviously saw that Musemeelin had blackened his face, held a rifle, and carried his tomahawk on his belt.

"Where is my horse?" Musemeelin asked angrily.

Armstrong: "He will come by and by."

Musemeelin: "I want him now."

Armstrong: "You shall have him. Come, let us go to that fire ... and let us talk and smoke together."

Musemeelin: "Go along, then."

Armstrong: "I am coming."

As Armstrong walked toward the fire, Musemeelin raised his rifle and shot him in the back. Gravely wounded, the trader fell forward. "Musemeelin then took his hatchet and struck it into Armstrong's head, and said, 'Give me my horse, I tell you.'"

Jimmy ran off when he saw Musemeelin strike Armstrong, but came back in a while.

Musemeelin ordered Jimmy and John to help him bury the trader's body and to throw the other corpses into the Juniata. He also cautioned them sternly against ever telling anyone about the killings.

They dug a shallow grave for Armstrong then dumped the other bodies in the river.

Musemeelin then directed his companions to load the trader's goods and furs on the pack horses. While John and Jimmy did this, Musemeelin took Armstrong's ax and cut three notches in the trunk of an oak tree near Armstrong's grave. When the horses were loaded, the three led them toward a nearby hill where Musemeelin said they would hide Armstrong's merchandise.

As they walked, Musemeelin told them that "there were a great many Indians hunting about that place," and "if they should happen to meet with any," they would kill them to protect the secret of Armstrong's murder.

Musemeelin took the lead, and this gave Jimmy and John a chance to talk privately. They agreed that they wouldn't help Musemeelin kill anybody else and that they would "run away as soon as they could." They also decided that despite Musemeelin's stated intentions, they themselves would refuse to harm any Indians that they might meet.

When they reached the place where Musemeelin intended to stash the stolen goods, they unloaded the pack horses, and Musemeelin began opening the bundles. As he did so, he offered to give John and Jimmy some bundles of furs, but the two young Indians declined Musemeelin's offer. "They told him that as they had already sold their skins, and everybody knew they had nothing. They would certainly be charged with a black action, were they to bring any goods to the town, and therefore they would not accept of any, but promised, nevertheless, not to betray him."

Musemeelin rebuked them sharply. "Now," he said, "I know what you were talking about when you stayed so far behind."

This frightened John and Jimmy, and they took the bundles that Musemeelin had offered. By now it had started to rain, and the three men heaped everything else in a pile and covered it to protect it from the weather. Then they returned to Musemeelin's cabin.

When the weather cleared, Jimmy started walking back to Shamokin, but John stayed on to help Musemeelin hide Armstrong's goods. Along the way they met several others Indians, and Musemeelin "said he had killed Jack Armstrong and taken … his horse." He threatened to kill anyone who exposed him. He also offered to share the loot. Two of these Indians helped Musemeelin and John bury the goods, but wouldn't accept anything from Musemeelin.

After Jimmy finished telling Allumapees and his companions about the murders, the chief went to confer with Shikellamy. They "agreed to secure the murderers, and deliver them up to the white people. Then a great noise arose among the Delaware Indians, and some were afraid of their lives, and went into the woods," Weiser said in his report. "Not one cared to meddle with Musemeelin."

When this happened, Shikellamy and Allumapees decided to send for Conrad Weiser and "got one of the Tutelo Indians to write a letter to me to desire me to come to Shamokin in all haste, that the Indians were much dissatisfied in mind. This letter was brought to my house by four Delaware Indians sent express." But Weiser was in Philadelphia when the messengers reached at his farm at Tulpehocken, about fifteen miles northwest of Reading and nearly seventy miles from the Forks of the Susquehanna.

The letter was waiting for him when he returned from Philadelphia several days later. It described the events at Shamokin, and when Weiser realized that "none of the Indians of the Six Nations had been down," he decided not to take any action. "I did not care to meddle with Delaware Indian affairs, and stayed at home till I received the governor's orders to go, which was about two weeks after," Weiser said.

Making the Arrests

Meanwhile, word spread throughout Shamokin that the chiefs intended to arrest Musemeelin and John, the son of Neshaleeny, and to take the two down to the white settlements. The Delawares reacted by making a tremendous commotion, but Shikellamy's sons pressured them to take the two into custody. Finally, "four or five of the Delawares made Musemeelin and the other young man prisoners, and tied them both." This caused such a ruckus that Allumapees, "in danger of being killed, fled to Shikellamy and begged his protection." A full twenty-four hours passed, and none of the Delaware men were willing to transport the prisoners to the white settlements south of the Blue Mountain.

"At last Shikellamy's son, Jack, went to the Delawares, most of them being drunk as they had been for several days, and told them to deliver the prisoners to Alexander Armstrong," who lived along the Susquehanna about thirty-five miles south of Shamokin. The Delawares feared Armstrong, and refused to do this, but Jack Shikellamy pressed them. He eventually agreed "to assist them, and accordingly he and his brother and some of the Delawares went with two canoes and carried them off."

At this point, James Berry makes his third appearance in the story. He was one of the white men who went along with the Armstrong brothers to search for the bodies of the Indian traders. He was also the man to whom Jack Armstrong had either given or sold Musemeelin's horse. In this segment of the record, the Shikellamy brothers "in going down the river" with their prisoners stopped at Berry's house. Berry had known the Neshaleeny boy and said to him: "I am sorry to see you in such a condition, I have known you from a boy, and always loved you."

Berry's comment had a powerful impact on the young man, who "seemed to be very much struck to the heart, and said, 'I have said nothing yet, but I will tell all. Let all the Indians come up, and the white people also. They shall hear it.'"

With his captors and Berry present, John Neshaleeny said to Musemeelin: "Now I am going to die for your wickedness. You have killed all the three white men. I never did intend to kill any of them."

Musemeelin replied angrily: "It is true, I have killed them. I am a man, you are a coward. It is a great satisfaction to me to have killed them. I will die with joy for having killed a great rogue and his companions."

When Musemeelin said this, the Indians released the younger prisoner from custody. The Shikellamy brothers and the Delawares continued downriver with Musemeelin, who was eventually lodged in the jail at Lancaster.

Conrad Weiser Arrives

Even though the frontier remained peaceful, tensions were still building when Weiser arrived in Shamokin in early May. He told Allumapees and the Delawares "in the presence of Shikellamy and a few more of the Six Nations" that Governor Thomas knew about the killings and had sent him "to demand those that had been concerned with Musemeelin in murdering John Armstrong, Woodworth Arnold, and

Hand-drawn portrait of Conrad Weiser, artist unknown.

James Smith." The governor also wanted "their bodies … searched for, and decently buried." The Delawares also needed to recover the goods that had been stolen from Armstrong. These needed to be "restored without fraud" to the trader's relatives.

The governor's message "was delivered (to) them by me in the Mohawk language, and interpreted into Delaware by Andrew, Madame Montour's son," Weiser said.

In turn, Allumapees acknowledged "that we, the Delaware Indians, by the instigation of the evil spirit, have murdered Jack Armstrong and his men. We have transgressed, and we are ashamed to look up." Regarding Musemeelin, the chief said, "We have taken the murderer and delivered him to the relations of the deceased, to be dealt with according to his works." He also promised to make full restitution. If the Delawares were unable to return all the merchandise, "whatever is wanting, we will make up with skins."

As for the murder victims themselves, "the dead bodies are buried. It is certain that John Armstrong was buried by the murderer, and the other two by those that searched for them, Our hearts are in mourning, and we are in a dismal condition, and cannot say anything at present."

When it was Shikellamy's turn to speak, he declared that "Musemeelin has certainly murdered the three white men himself, and upon his bare accusation of Neshaleeny's son, which was nothing but spite … Neshaleeny's son was seized, and made a prisoner. Our cousins, the Delaware Indians, being then drunk, in particular Allumapees, never examined things, but made an innocent person prisoner, which gave a great deal of disturbance amongst us."

The Iroquois chief at this point described the circumstances in which Musemeelin had confessed to committing all three murders himself. He said that he hoped that Governor Thomas "will not insist to have either of the two young men in prison or condemned to die: it is not with Indians as with white people, to put people in prison on suspicion or trifles. Indians must first be found guilty of a crime, then judgment is given and immediately executed."

Shikellamy said that his people wanted to see "good friendship and harmony continue" between the Indians and the Pennsylvanians. "That we may live long together is the hearty desire of your brethren, the Indians of the United Six Nations present at Shamokin," he said.

Thus, the case of the Jack Armstrong murders began a new phase, and a sullen Musemeelin became the only prisoner from Shamokin to wind up in prison.

By April 22, a dejected but suddenly talkative Musemeelin was sitting in the Lancaster jail awaiting transport to Philadelphia when he surprised one of his jailers, Thomas Cookson, by telling about the killings.

"He speaks English well," Cookson said in a letter to the governor.

As the prisoner told it, Jimmy/Billy and John, son of Neshaleeny, had accompanied Musemeelin on a hunt during the autumn of 1743. "That about the middle of February last, John and Billy went down to a place that had been settled by a Dutchman on Juniata Creek (*sic*), and there saw J. Armstrong, and his two men, going back into the woods with goods, and had some discourse with them."

When the Indians met up with Musemeelin a while after this, they "told him that J. Armstrong and two men were going into ye woods with goods, and that they had a mind to kill them, and asked him to join with them, to which he readily assented." It took the three men about two days to catch up with Armstrong. When they did, Musemeelin "went up to J. Armstrong and asked him for some wampum he had pledged with him, or satisfaction for it, and also a horse that he said Armstrong had taken from him in ye fall ... (on) account of a small debt due to him."

Musemeelin told the jailer: "Some hot words arose upon this, and Armstrong took up a stake and struck him, on which he struck Armstrong with his tomahawk on the temple and he dropped dead on ye spot. Arnold, one of Armstrong's men, attempted to make a blow at Musemeelin with an axe, but he retired to his gun where he had lodged it ready loaded and shot him, and afterwards wounded him in the head with his tomahawk."

The prisoner also told Cookson that John Neshaleeny killed James Smith with his tomahawk, and that the men buried Armstrong's body and threw the other bodies into the Juniata. He asserted that later the Indians dug a hole to stash Armstrong's goods, and that John and Billy each kept some woolen trade blankets.

Musemeelin also remarked that "he thinks it very hard that the other Indian should be released, and that the reason assigned by Shikellamy's sons was not ye true reason" that they let him go. He charged that Jack and his brother were actually "apprehensive of the resentment of Neshaleeny's friends against their father" for turning the son over to the white people. The prisoner asserted that the Shikellamies "thought it most prudent to release him and deliver up Musemeelin only," Cookson said.

After reading Cookson's letter, Governor Thomas ordered Musemeelin moved to the jail in Philadelphia.

End of the Trail

John, son of Neshaleeny, and Jimmy/Billy subsequently traveled to Philadelphia, presumably on foot, and gave evidence against Musemeelin, who was hanged in mid-November. Two newspapers—the Pennsylvania Gazette and the Pennsylvania Journal—each carried brief items about the Indian's execution.

Epilogue

Someone invariably gets to have the last word. In this case, it was Conrad Weiser. In a 1746 letter to a friend, he said that after Musemeelin had been sent off to prison, but prior to his execution, Weiser and other representatives of Governor Thomas who had been involved in the Armstrong affair were invited to attend a feast in Shamokin.

The highlight of the event occurred when "the eldest of the chiefs made a speech, in which he said: 'That by a great misfortune, three of the brethren, the white men, had been killed by an Indian; that nevertheless the sun was not set (meaning there was no war), it had only been somewhat darkened by a small cloud ..." But the dark cloud was now gone.

The speeches were made after the dinner—in Weiser's words, "after we had in great silence devoured a fat bear."

Actually, that was Weiser's next-to-the-last word. In July 1747, in writing to Richard Peters, secretary of the colony, about Shikellamy and Indian affairs generally, Weiser again brought up the Armstrong case. Here's what he said:

"When an Indian in his own judgment thinks himself wronged by somebody, more especially by the white people, he will never forgive and he is apt to revenge himself, and urged to do it by his country people. John Armstrong, the poor man, had warning sufficient to persuade him to do the Indians justice, but covetousness prevented him. At last he paid too dear for his faults."

If you think about it, so did Musemeelin, although it was vengeance rather than greed that took the Indian to the gallows.

Delaware Hunters Warred Against Bears

Late 1700s

During the late 1700s, the Delaware Indians regarded themselves at war with the black bears that inhabited the forests of Pennsylvania and Ohio. Although they regarded whitetail deer as game animals, they didn't see bears in the same light. In the Indians' view, the bears belonged to a tribe that was at war with the Delawares. When individual hunters went out after bears, they regarded themselves as warriors going into combat against hostile warriors belonging to an enemy tribe.

This concept might be difficult for twenty-first century Americans—hunters as well as non-hunters—to grasp, but there's ample documentation to support it. For instance, the Rev. John Heckewelder was a Moravian missionary who lived among the Delawares for several decades, spoke their language, and studied their customs. He was present one day when a Delaware hunter shot a large bear and injured it severely.

"The animal fell and set up a most plaintive cry," the missionary said. "The hunter instead of giving him another shot, stood up close to him, and addressed him in these words: 'Hark ye, bear. You are a coward and no warrior as you pretend to be. Were you a warrior, you would show it by your firmness and not cry and whimper like an old woman.'"

Heckewelder was surprised when the hunter continued to taunt the bear. "Had you conquered me, I would have borne it with courage and died like a brave warrior," the Indian said. "But you, bear, sit here and

Portrait of Rev, John Heckewelder from "Howe's Historical Collections of Ohio Volume II", p. 690 (1907).

cry, and disgrace your tribe by your cowardly conduct."

As Heckewelder recounted the incident later, after the hunter had killed the animal, "I asked him how he thought that poor animal could understand what he said to it?

"Oh!" the Indian replied. "The bear understood me very well. Did you not observe how ashamed he looked while I was upbraiding him?"

Heckewelder said he witnessed a similar incident along the Ohio River that involved a white man, William Wells, who had been raised by Indians living along the Wabash River. While hunting one day, Wells dropped a large bear with one shot from his flintlock rifle. Unable to move, "the animal cried piteously," the missionary said. As Heckewelder watched, "The young man went up to him, and with seemingly great earnestness, addressed him in the Wabash language, now and then giving him a slight stroke on the nose with his ram-rod."

When Heckewelder later asked Wells what he had said to the bear, the hunter replied, "I have upbraided him for acting the part of a coward. I told him that he knew the fortune of war, that one or the other of us must have fallen; that it was his fate to be conquered, and he ought to die like a man, like a hero, and not like an old woman."

He told the beast "that if the case had been reversed, and I had fallen into the power of my enemy, I would not have disgraced my nation as he did, but would have died with firmness and courage, as becomes a true warrior."

Hunting While Traveling

When Delaware Indians traveled long distances, the men frequently provided fresh meat for everyone on the trip by hunting during the journey, Heckewelder said. The travelers frequently included men, women, and children. The hunters would rise early and head out in the direction that the group would be going that day.

"Some of the young men are sent out to hunt by the way, who, when they have killed a deer, bear, or other animal, bring it to the path, ready to be taken away by those who are coming along, often with horses, to the place of encampment, when they all meet at night," Heckewelder said.

When hunters shot an animal, they field dressed it and carried it to the trail over which their companions would be coming. They hung the meat on low-hanging tree branches along the trail. "These young men make a kind of sun-dial, in order to inform those who are coming of the time of day it was at the time of their arrival and departure," Heckewelder said.

They drew a circle in the earth, then stuck a stick two or three feet long in the center, "with its upper end bent towards that spot in the horizon where the sun stood at the time of their arrival or departure."

The hunters had their own individual sign or mark, "which they make on the trees, where they strike off from the path to their hunting grounds or place of encampment, which is often at the distance of many miles," he said.

The Hunter's Role Wasn't Sport

For native men, hunting for deer, bear, and other animals valued for their meat and skins was an occupation, not a sport or recreation, and they approached it as such. "The hunter prefers going out with his gun on an empty stomach," Heckewelder said. "He says that hunger stimulates him to exertion by reminding him continually of his wants, whereas a full stomach makes a hunter easy, careless, and lazy."

There was considerable competition for game in the forest. Other Indian hunters and wolves ranged through the same woods looking for game. This meant that a successful hunter often had to put in a long day's work. As Heckewelder reported, "Many a day passes over their heads that they have not met with any kind of game, nor consequently tasted a morsel of victuals; still they go on with their chase, in hopes of being able to carry some provisions home, and do not give up the pursuit until it is so dark that they can see no longer."

Here's a domestic scene of the type that Heckewelder saw repeatedly during his decades of missionary service:

"The hunter who happens to have no meat in the house will be off and in the woods before daylight, and strive to be in again for breakfast with a deer, turkey, goose, bear, or raccoon, or some other game then in season. Meanwhile, his wife has pounded her corn, now boiling on the fire, and baked her bread, which gives them a good breakfast. If, however, the husband is not returned by ten o'clock in the forenoon, the family take their meal by themselves, and his share is put aside for him when he comes home."

Delaware women did most of the cooking. "Their roasting is done by running a wooden spit through the meat, sharpened at each end, which they place near the fire, and occasionally turn. They broil on clean coals, drawn off from the fire for that purpose," Heckewelder said.

"They are fond of dried venison, pounded in a mortar and dipped in bear's oil."

William Penn Presides over Witchcraft Trial

February 1683

Margaret Mattson, an early Pennsylvanian, had the reputation of being a witch. One day she hexed a neighbor's cow, but it was the wrong cow. Not to worry. She remedied her error by moving the spell to a bovine belonging to another neighbor.

At least, that's what an accuser testified at Mattson's 1683 trial in Philadelphia. Official records of the Pennsylvania colony disclose that proprietor William Penn himself presided, and that Penn's attorney general prosecuted her.

James Saunderling told Penn's court that "his mother told him that she (Mattson) bewitched her cow, but afterwards said it was a mistake, and that her cow should do well again, for it was not her cow, but another person's that should die."

Mattson stood trial on two specific charges: First, that she had the reputation of being a witch; and, second, that she cast evil spells on livestock belonging to people living in the Ridley Creek settlements southwest of Philadelphia.

Colonial authorities took the case seriously. At a February 12 hearing, they ordered Mattson's husband, Neels Mattson, "to enter into a recognizance of 50 pounds for his wife's appearance before this board" for trial on February 27.

The trial began with a reading of the indictment against her. Lasse Cock, a Swedish settler who sat on Penn's Provincial Council, was appointed to interpret for Mattson, a Swedish woman who didn't speak English. She pleaded not guilty.

Engraving of a colonial-era witch trial.

A second witness, Henry Drystreet, testified that he "was told 20 years ago that the prisoner at the bar was a witch and that several cows were bewitched by her."

A third witness, Charles Ashcom, testified that Mattson's own daughter told him that "she sold her cattle ... because her mother had bewitched them."

If such hearsay wasn't convincing, consider the testimony of a woman named Annakey Coolin. A calf that she and her husband were raising suddenly "died, as they thought, by witchcraft," she said. Apparently the Coolinses believed the meat would be safe to eat if they could somehow rid the carcass of the spell. According to an official extract of the trial, "her husband took the heart ... and boiled it."

While the heart was cooking, Mattson "came in and asked them what they were doing. They said, boiling off flesh," Coolin told the court. Mattson retorted they would have better results if "they had boiled the bones," the witness reported.

Engraving of the proprietor, William Penn.

The record of the trial indicates that Coolin also alleged that Mattson had possibly bewitched some geese at the Coolin farm.

When Mattson had the opportunity to testify in her own defense, she acknowledged that she had come along the creek to the Coolin farm in her canoe, but denied "Coolin's attestation concerning the geese ... saying she was never out of her canoe." Nor did she ever say "any such things regarding the calf's heart."

Mattson flatly denied being a witch, contended that all the charges against her were false, and declared "that the witnesses speak only by hearsay."

At one point, Mattson rebutted Ashcom's assertions regarding her daughter. "Where is my daughter?" Mattson asked. "Let her come and say so."

The trial proceeded rapidly. Deliberations didn't take long after William Penn gave the jury of twelve men their charge.

According to colonial records: "The jury went forth, and upon their return brought her in guilty of having the common fame of a witch, but not guilty in manner and form as she stands indicted."

Her sentence was a lenient one: her husband and son, Anthony Neelson, each entered into "a recognizance of 50 pounds apiece for the good behavior of Margaret Mattson for six months."

Footnote: In a 1908 article titled "A Study in Social History," author Amelia Mott Gummere wrote: "Margaret Mattson lived upon her husband's plantation on the Delaware, near Crum Creek, in Ridley Township, now Delaware County. She remained for long in local legend, the "Witch of Ridley Creek."

Shikellamy, Bishop Negotiate for Gun Repairs

January 1748

During the 1740s, Indians living along the Susquehanna River did a lot of hunting and trapping so they could sell furs to white traders whose packhorses carried manufactured goods into the region.

"The country was populous with Indians, and a trader with a train of twenty or thirty packhorses could in a very short time dispose of his wares," a frontiersman told visitors Joseph Powell and John Cammerhoff in January 1748.

Traveling on foot, Cammerhoff and Powell were headed upriver to the Moravian mission at the Indian town of Shamokin. They had stayed overnight at the settler's house, which was a short distance north of the Wisconisco Creek, near present-day Millersburg.

"Our host was acquainted with our brethren at Shamokin, and had assisted them in transporting their supplies," Cammerhoff wrote in his journal.

Located at the Susquehanna's confluence, the native town sprawled across parts of present-day Sunbury, Northumberland, and Packers Island. The people living there were mainly Delaware, Iroquois, and Tutelo Indians. Before migrating to Pennsylvania, the Tutelos had lived in Virginia and the Carolinas.

Outside the jurisdiction of the Pennsylvania colony, Shamokin was also the base of Shikellamy, an Oneida chief who represented the Iroquois Confederacy in the Susquehanna Valley and who functioned as a sort of territorial governor.

The Moravians had established their mission and a blacksmith's shop at Shamokin in 1747. Not only did

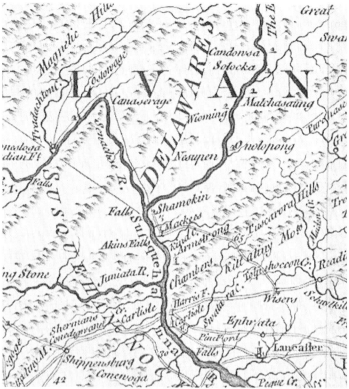

Section of the 1756 map of Pennsylvania with Shamokin (modern day Sunbury) in the center.

the smith make everyday objects at his forge, but he also repaired firearms that the Indians used for hunting. "Our smith is kept constantly employed, many Indians coming from a great distance," reported Cammerhoff, who was bishop of the Moravian Church in Bethlehem.

By this time, many native hunters had stopped using bows and arrows and had switched over to flintlock rifles, which they obtained from the traders in exchange for furs. The traders also supplied them with bullets and gunpowder.

When the bishop met with Shikellamy at the mission, the chief asked if the smith could accept a variety of animal skins as payment for fixing an Indian's gun.

"So far the smith has only taken deer skins in compensation for his work," Shikellamy said. "Cannot he also take raccoon, fox, wildcat, and otter skins at the market price? Some of us are old and can no more follow the deer. T'girhitontie (the bishop) and his brethren could as well take other skins and sell them, and in this way the smith will be paid for all his work."

The bishop explained that he wasn't willing to make the change: The blacksmith and missionaries "are no traders, nor do they traffic in furs. This is not their business, and hence the smith cannot take all kinds of skins. The deer-skins T'girhitontie uses to make breeches, caps, gloves, etcetera, for his brethren. But as we love you, the smith may sometimes take otter, raccoon and fox skins, when they are good."

A little later, Shikellamy asked: "Cannot the smith also take bear and elk skins for his work?"

The bishop replied: "He can take as many bear skins as are brought, for he and his brethren need them to sleep on. But it is best that he be paid in deer skins, for T'girhitontie and his people are no traders."

It's significant that Shikellamy didn't ask if the smith could accept buffalo skins. Shamokin-based hunters ranged over a wide territory to the north and west of the Susquehanna confluence. The omission suggests either that there weren't any bison in the forests or that the Indians were deliberately not killing them. Place names such as Buffalo Creek in Union County continue to fuel legends that bison once roamed the West Branch Valley.

David Zeisberger, a Moravian missionary who served in the Shamokin mission, eventually spent many years in Ohio and wrote extensively about Indians west of the Allegheny Mountains, where eastern wood bison were once plentiful.

"The best time for the chase is in the fall, when the game is fat and the hides are good," Zeisberger wrote. "The deer, which are most sought ..., have the best skins," he said.

He added, "Elk and buffalo they shoot little and rarely, as the hides are too heavy and of little value, and if they shoot one of these animals now and again, most of the meat is left lying in the woods, where it is consumed by wolves or other wild animals or birds."

Before Indian hunters in Ohio began using firearms, "their weapons were the bow and arrow and a wooden club," Zeisberger wrote. "Shields they bore made of hardened buffalo leather and presenting a convex surface without, while being hollow within. The curved outer surface they held toward the enemy and before their own breasts and faces in order that arrows discharged at them, striking the curved surface, would glance off and go to the side. With the left hand they held both shield and bow, and with the right they drew the bow and held the arrow."

The missionary reported that there were occasions when Indians even domesticated a few buffalo. "One that I have seen was a yearling, raised by the Indians and quite tame," Zeisberger said. He added: "If a buffalo cow is shot, its calf ... will stand quietly by until the huntsman has skinned its dam (mother) and then follow him into his hut, stay at his fire, and not leave him. That this is true, I have living witnesses enough about me to testify."

Smallpox, Starvation Hit the Susquehanna

July 1748

Starvation and disease visited the Indian villages along the upper Susquehanna River during the summer of 1748.

On July 25, two missionaries traveling along the North Branch found the natives at Wapwallopen so hungry that they "boiled the bark of trees for food."

Two weeks earlier, the two Moravians—David Zeisberger and John Martin Mack—had found similar conditions among the Indians when they traveled along the West Branch.

On July 11, for instance, they arrived at an Indian village on Great Island across from modern Lock Haven, and found people suffering from smallpox "in all of the huts ... in one hung a kettle in which grass was being stewed, which they ate with avidity."

Mack and Zeisberger were stationed at the Moravian mission in present-day Sunbury, then known as Shamokin. They kept a daily journal of their West Branch trip, which began on July 9.

Around noon on July 10, they reached the village of Otstonwakin (near Montoursville), "which we found deserted."

They camped along the trail that night and wrote the next day that they had been "tormented by punks (gnats) and mosquitoes despite the five fires between which we lay down to sleep."

At midday they came to a place along the river where there were a number of Indian huts. All were deserted. They went over to an island, "where we found a number of huts, but not a soul about," the Moravians said.

Engraving of David Zeisberger, from a portrait painted at the age of forty.

The grass and weeds were very high, and Mack climbed a tree to get a better view. He saw an Indian near the point of the island, and the missionaries walked over there. "Here we found a hut in which was an old woman and some others down with the smallpox."

Zeisberger and Mack asked where all the Indians had gone. They learned that many had died from smallpox and that others had gone to the white settlements in southeastern Pennsylvania in hope of getting food there.

Most of the natives who lived along this section of the river were Delawares. One man "was very friendly and pointed out the way to Great Island, but regretted he had nothing to give us to eat," the missionaries said.

The travelers reached Great Island towards evening. Although they found a number of Indians there, "most of the men had been driven away by famine," they said. "We asked whether we could lodge in a hut overnight, were cordially received, and a bear skin spread for us to sleep on, but could not obtain anything to eat."

The people living on the island included Shawnees and Cayugas.

In the morning "our host brought us some dried venison, and we in turn gave his child some of our bread, for which he was very thankful," they said.

As the day progressed, Zeisberger and Mack visited other Indians in the neighborhood. At one point, they came upon some people "who had just returned from the woods, and who shared with us the unripe grapes they had gathered."

As the missionaries prepared to walk back to Shamokin, "our host gave us some dried venison, and in return we gave him and his wife some needles and thread."

The missionaries returned to Shamokin a few days later, and on July 22 headed up the North Branch, also on foot. July 23 was a rainy day, and their clothing was wet by the time they reached the Indian town at Nescopeck in the evening. "We found few at home, but were taken into a hut where we dried ourselves and supperless retired to rest."

The next morning "our host cooked some wild beans of which we partook. We gave the old man in turn some of our bread."

Road Cutters Hacked through 200 Miles of Forest

May 1755

Using twenty-first century roads, a motorist can easily retrace Maj. Gen. Edward Braddock's 1755 route from Alexandria, Va., to Pittsburgh, Pa., in less than a day. This distance is approximately 260 miles.

From Alexandria, the general took his army to Frederick, Md., then to Winchester, Va., and Cumberland, Md., before finally marching toward Pittsburgh. Actually, he only got as close as Braddock, a modern borough named for him and situated about ten miles from the confluence of the Monongahela and Allegheny rivers, where Fort DuQuesne was located.

French soldiers had built the fort in 1754 after they had forced Virginians to surrender their fortified trading post at the site. The French and the British were at war, and England had sent Braddock to drive the French back to Canada. His orders called for him to destroy Fort DuQuesne.

Implementing Braddock's plan entailed marching twenty-five hundred soldiers two hundred miles through heavily forested mountains that offered an assortment of narrow trails that a horse and rider could use, but lacked graded roads and bridges wide enough and otherwise suitable for horse-drawn wagons and cannon. To reach his objective, Braddock would have to literally hack his way through old-growth forests and construct a road over which horses could pull both artillery and supply wagons loaded with food, ammunition, and other essentials. Such a rustic highway would need to be twelve feet wide, just enough to allow the scores of wagons and artillery in the baggage train to proceed in single file. Once under

Portrait of Edward Braddock.

way, the soldiers would also be forced to protect the cumbersome convoy against raids by small groups of enemy Indians who specialized in attacking suddenly, then withdrawing just as suddenly.

Braddock and his aides realized that to accomplish all this, they would need hundreds of farm wagons and more than a thousand pack horses. Early on, one of the expedition's key officers, Sir John St. Clair, "assured the general that ... he had been informed of a great number of Dutch (German) settlers, at the foot of a mountain called the Blue Ridge, who would undertake to carry by the hundred the provisions and stores." So reported Captain Robert Orme, Braddock's chief aide. St. Clair told Braddock "that he believed he could provide ... two hundred wagons and fifteen hundred carrying horses to be at Fort Cumberland by the 1st of May."

Despite St. Clair's assurances, the army's difficulty in securing adequate transport soon began to show itself. By early April 1755, the general was ready to leave Alexandria and head to Frederick, Md., "but few wagons or teams were yet come to remove the artillery," Orme reported. "He then sent an express to Sir John St. Clair informing him of it, and in a few days set out for Frederick in Maryland leaving Lt. Col. Gage with four companies of the 44th regiment, who was ordered to dispatch the powder and artillery as fast as any horses or wagons should arrive." As it happened, a fortnight passed before Gage had the transportation he needed to move out.

Braddock headed for Frederick, some fifty miles northwest of Alexandria, confident that a supply of provisions would be waiting. Instead, he was dismayed to arrive and find "the troops in great want of provision; no cattle was laid in there," Orme reported. Nor had any wagons been "provided for the Maryland side of the Potomac. The general applied to Governor Sharpe, who promised above one hundred." When Braddock pressed Sharpe to arrange for food for the soldiers, "the governor afforded the general no assistance, upon which the general was obliged to send round the country to buy cattle for the subsistence of the troops."

Benjamin Franklin, representing the Pennsylvania colony, came to Frederick to meet with the general. Braddock lost little time in asking Franklin to "contract in Pennsylvania for 150 wagons and 1,500 carrying horses upon the easiest terms, to join him at Fort Cumberland by the 10th of May, if possible,"

Orme wrote. Fort Cumberland was nearly 150 miles away from Alexandria. "Mr. Franklin procured the number of wagons, and about 500 horses."

Deep into the campaign, Braddock took stock of his fleet of wagons. As Orme reported later, the general told his officers "that he found by his returns that he had not above 40 wagons over and above the 150 he had got from Pennsylvania, and that the number of carrying horses did not exceed 600, which were insufficient to carry 70 days flour and 50 days meat, which he was of opinion was the least he could march with without running great risks of being reduced to the utmost distress."

The great forests of Maryland and Pennsylvania posed another huge difficulty. Pastures were few, and once the army passed Fort Cumberland, there weren't any supply stations provisioned with hay, oats, and other foods for the livestock. Consequently, "most of the horses which brought up the train were either lost, or carried home by their owners, the nature of the country making it impossible to avoid this fatal inconvenience, the whole being a continued forest for several hundred miles without enclosures or bounds by which horses can be secured. They must be turned into the woods for their subsistence, and feed upon leaves and young shoots of trees. Many projects, such as belts, hobbles, &c., were tried, but none of these were a security against the wildness of the country and the knavery of the people we were obliged to employ," Orme reported. "By these means we lost our horses almost as fast as we could collect them, and those which remained grew very weak, so we found ourselves every day less able to undertake the extraordinary march we were to perform."

Another obstacle presented itself as the army marched inland. In at least one case, an unscrupulous contractor sent improperly preserved meat for Fort Cumberland from the Maryland settlements. Braddock had arranged for Governor Sharpe "to salt a quantity of beef for the use of the Maryland troops," Orme

Benjamin Franklin

reported. "It was no sooner brought to camp, but it was condemned to be buried by a survey. The surveyors reported that it had no pickle, and that it was put into dry casks, which could never have contained any."

This shipment arrived at a time when the troops at Fort Cumberland needed both flour and beef, so Braddock "sent away that night 30 wagons with a captain's detachment to Winchester for provisions over 60 miles of mountainous and rocky country; and also 300 carrying horses for flour ..."

Braddock had been ready to leave Fort Cumberland and realized that it would take seven days for the wagons to make the one hundred-mile roundtrip to Winchester with fresh provisions. Rather than wait a week, he split his force, and sent six hundred men on ahead.

With Major Chapman in command, the column moved out at daybreak on May 30. Two miles from the fort, the soldiers had to climb a steep mountain, where three hundred men belonging to a company of miners had spent several days in cutting a road across the ridge. "It was night before the whole baggage (train) had got over a mountain about two miles from the camp," Orme reported. "The ascent and descent were almost a perpendicular rock; three wagons were entirely destroyed ... and many more were extremely shattered."

Although the distance between Fort Cumberland and Fort DuQuesne was only 110 miles, Braddock's army required the entire month of June and nearly a third of July to get within striking distance of the French post.

The lack of horses created an enormous challenge. The general had split his army into two groups: the advance force, which intended to attack and capture the French fort, and the much slower supply train. The deeper the advance force moved into the forest, the farther away it got from the supply wagons. In turn, the farther the baggage wagons advanced into the wilderness, the less food was available for the horses pulling them. Growing numbers of horses began to starve. "They die so fast that when they (soldiers in the supply train) march, they cannot draw above half the wagons, so when they come to their (camp) ground, they are obliged to send the horses back for the remainder of the wagons, which delays them so much that they cannot overtake us," wrote an officer's servant in the forward unit.

On June 25 the column passed Great Meadows and camped for the night about two miles to the west. "About a quarter of a mile (east) from this camp, we were obliged to let our carriages down a hill with tackles, which made it later than usual before we got to our ground," Orme reported.

Braddock wanted the advance force to march rapidly and to capture Fort DuQuesne before reinforcements from Canada could strengthen its garrison. One immediate consequence of the growing distance between the supply train and the strike force was that soldiers in the advance began to receive short rations. The shortage became so pressing that when the battle between Braddock's army and the French

Braddock's defeat.

and their Indian allies occurred on July 9, some of the British soldiers hadn't had any food to eat for two days.

The question of wagons remained an issue for Braddock right up to and after his death in mid-July. As his command disintegrated around him throughout the afternoon of July 9, Braddock insisted on staying close to the front and did what he could to prevent the French victory. Even when a gunshot toppled the general, he refused to leave the field. He had been shot through the arm and body. In the end, the wounded commander, still conscious, "was put in a wagon" and transported off the field, an anonymous officer

The burial of General Braddock.

reported. Evacuated across the Monongahela, he rejoined the remnants of his army, and shortly thereafter, "the general sent Mr. Washington to Colonel Dunbar with orders to send wagons for the wounded, some provision and hospital stores," Captain Orme said in his official report.

The general died on July 13 along the stretch of road that crossed the Great Meadows. His soldiers deliberately dug his grave in the middle of the road. After the burial, Braddock's officers had all the soldiers, horses, and wagons pass over the grave. This was done to prevent the Indians and French from finding and desecrating the general's body.

Washington Invites Andrew Montour to Virginia

September 1755

In late 1755 when George Washington found himself charged with defending the Virginia frontier against French and Indian marauders, he turned to Andrew Montour for help.

Writing on September 19 from a frontier fort in Maryland, Washington informed Montour that he had assumed command of the Virginia forces, and "I am ... very desirous of seeing you here.... Bring some Indians along with you.... If you think it proper to bring Mrs. Montour along with you, she shall ... be provided for."

The son of Madame Catherine Montour, Andrew, was part French and part Iroquois. He had spent many years in the Susquehanna River Valley and could speak English, French, Delaware, Iroquois, and perhaps other languages. He became an interpreter, but also distinguished himself as a guide and a warrior.

Washington and Montour had known each other for several years, and Washington's letters make it clear that he sought Montour's services as a backwoods fighter.

When French soldiers ventured into the Upper Ohio River Valley in the early 1750s, Pennsylvania sent Montour into the region with diplomatic messages for Indians who had ties to Pennsylvania and white Indian traders based in the Pennsylvania colony.

Montour soon encountered Washington. In 1754, when the French evicted Virginia traders from present-day Pittsburgh, Washington and other Virginia soldiers erected a stockade post, Fort Necessity, about seventy-five miles southeast of Pittsburgh. Montour was the

48

Andrew Montour

captain of a small company of frontiersmen who helped defend the fort.

The French forced Washington to surrender and then withdraw from the region, but both Montour and Washington returned to the territory the following summer, Washington as an aide to Gen. Edward Braddock, and Montour as the Virginia interpreter. Only a small number of Indians accompanied Braddock's army and took part in the July 9, 1755, battle known to history as Braddock's Defeat.

Braddock had planned to push the French out of the Ohio country, but the French and their Indian allies destroyed Braddock's force in a surprise confrontation along the Monongahela River about ten miles from present-day Pittsburgh. With Braddock mortally wounded, the professional soldiers from England fled the frontier, and Gov. Robert Dinwiddie put Washington in charge of defending the Virginia colony's frontier against the French and their Indian allies.

It was at this point that Washington reached out to Montour, who had returned to the Susquehanna.

When Montour didn't send a rapid response to Washington's first letter, the young colonel fired off a second one. "Dear Montour," he wrote on October 10. He urged Montour to bring "yourself, your family, and friendly Indians" to Virginia and help the colony protect its frontier. In signing the letter, Washington described himself as "your real friend."

A week later, Washington sent a trusted aide, Christopher Gist, to Harris's Ferry (present-day Harrisburg) to recruit influential Indians. Gist's instructions were concise: As soon as he arrived at Harris's, he was "to hire an Indian to go express to Captain Andrew Montour to whom you are to write, desiring him to come and assist you."

But Montour didn't go to Virginia. Instead, late October found him in the Indian town of Shamokin (modern Sunbury). In mid-October, pro-French Indians had massacred European farmers along Penns

Creek. When John Harris and other frontiersmen came up from present-day Harrisburg to survey the situation, they stopped at Shamokin and saw that many Indian men had blackened their faces for war. Returning home, they informed Conrad Weiser, the colony's Indian agent and an old friend of Montour, that, in Weiser's words, "Andrew Montour was there, painted as the rest."

Even so, Montour had advised Harris to return to Harrisburg by way of the river's east shore. Whites, he warned, who went down the west side would be ambushed by hostile Indians. The frontiersmen ignored Montour's warning. Consequently, many of them died in an ambush along Penns Creek near present-day Selinsgrove.

Survivors Describe Penns Creek Massacre

October 1755

Marie LeRoy awoke early on the morning of October 16, 1755, and began her daily chores on the family farm near Penns Creek.

Marie's father, Jean LeRoy, had a hired man who lived on the farm, and when he "went out to fetch the cows, he heard the Indians shooting six times," a witness reported later. "Soon after, eight of them came to the house, and killed Marie LeRoy's father with tomahawks. Her brother defended himself desperately for a time, but was at last overpowered. The Indians did not kill him, but took him prisoner, together with Marie LeRoy and a little girl, who was staying with the family."

Thus began an event known in Pennsylvania history as the Penns Creek Massacre, which occurred during the opening months of the French & Indian War. The LeRoy farm was located near Sweitzer's Run, a tributary of Penns Creek, a few miles southeast of Mifflinburg in Union County.

The LeRoys came from Switzerland and arrived in Pennsylvania in 1752, a time when forests still covered much of the region. They found farmland in southeastern Pennsylvania either already occupied by immigrants who had arrived before them, or too expensive for them to purchase.

Eventually, the LeRoys went northwest and crossed the Susquehanna River. They ventured into the woods along Penns Creek, then known as Mahanoy Creek. There were other settlers in the watershed, and since the LeRoys were the last to arrive, they went about twelve miles upstream before they found a suitable spot for a homestead.

Their nearest neighbor was Sebastian Leininger, a German immigrant who came to Pennsylvania in 1748. Leininger's daughter, Barbara, and Marie LeRoy became good friends. Both girls were fifteen at the time of the massacre.

The LeRoys built their cabin not far from an east-west path along the creek that Indians used when traveling between the Native American town of Shamokin (present-day Sunbury and Northumberland) and western Pennsylvania. The war party had followed this well-used trail as it came east from the Allegheny River. The LeRoy cabin had been the first European farm they had come to.

With the LeRoy cabin in flames, two warriors left to raid the Leininger farm. They found Barbara, her father, her brother, and her sister Regina at home, but Barbara's mother "had gone to the mill," presumably in present-day Selinsgrove.

The warriors barged into the cabin. "They demanded rum, but there was none in the house. Then they called for tobacco, which was given them. Having filled and smoked a pipe, they said: 'We are Allegheny Indians, and you're enemies. You must all die!' Thereupon they shot her father, tomahawked her brother, who was 20 years of age, took Barbara and her sister Regina prisoners, and conveyed them into the forest for about a mile. There they were soon joined by other Indians, with Marie LeRoy and the little girl."

Confident that there weren't any Pennsylvania soldiers nearby, the war party spent another day in the neighborhood so that the warriors could raid other homesteads along the creek. On the third day they departed, leaving thirteen dead settlers in their wake. Marie LeRoy and Barbara Leininger were among the twenty-eight prisoners they took to western Pennsylvania.

Years later, the girls gave a detailed account of their experiences. This article is based upon their account. They said that the warriors had divided the prisoners among the members of the war party and that they themselves had been given to a man named Galasko, who also had two horses stolen from the settlements.

Galasko, the girls said, "was tolerably kind, and allowed us to ride all the way, while he and the rest of the Indians walked." At one point Barbara saw a chance to escape, so she tried to ride away, "but she was almost immediately recaptured, and condemned to be burned alive."

The Indians gathered a lot of dry wood to make a large fire. Telling Barbara that she was about to die, "the savages gave her a French Bible, which they had taken from LeRoy's house, in order that she might prepare for death." When Barbara tearfully told them that she couldn't read French, "they gave her a German Bible," taken from another settler's cabin.

Barbara was crying very hard as the warriors set fire to the wood, "but a young Indian begged so earnestly for her life that she was pardoned, after having promised not to attempt to escape again, and to stop her crying."

After that, Barbara Leininger and Marie LeRoy lived with the Indians for three and a half years.

Today's travelers still use the eastern section of the Indian trail that led through the Penns Creek settlements. The path has been graded, paved, and renamed County Line Road. Union County is on the north side, and Snyder County, the south. But the road still descends through the same ravine that Indians once used to reach the Susquehanna River, opposite Sunbury.

The Indians deserted Shamokin less than a year after the massacre. Pennsylvania soldiers met no resistance when they arrived at the confluence of the Susquehanna in July 1756 and fortified the place. The cannons the soldiers brought upriver gave newly built Fort Augusta control of the river.

Chief Urges Pennsylvania to Build a Fort at Shamokin

February 1756

In the months before Pennsylvania soldiers began building Fort Augusta in July 1756, Indians and settlers alike had called for Gov. Robert H. Morris to erect such a fort.

Indians allied with the French in Canada had begun raiding English and German settlements in Central Pennsylvania. John Harris, a leader among whites living at present-day Harrisburg, was among the first to call for a fort along the Susquehanna River.

Reacting to the Penns Creek massacre in mid-October, Harris told the governor that Indians who remained loyal to the English might help in defending the colony "if we should raise a number of men immediately as will be able to take possession of some convenient place up Susquehanna, and build a strong fort ..."

Known as Shamokin, the Indian town at the Susquehanna's confluence was one of the biggest native settlements in Pennsylvania. It was also a logical place to build a fort.

Harris didn't specify where the fort should be built, but a few months later, the Belt of Wampum, a Seneca chief with close ties to both the Pennsylvania and Virginia colonies, reminded Pennsylvania officials on February 26, 1756, that at an earlier conference at Carlisle, "We advised you ... immediately to build a fort at Shamokin.... Such Indians as continue true to you want a place to come to and to live in security against your and their enemies—and to Shamokin when made strong they will come and bring their wives and children with them."

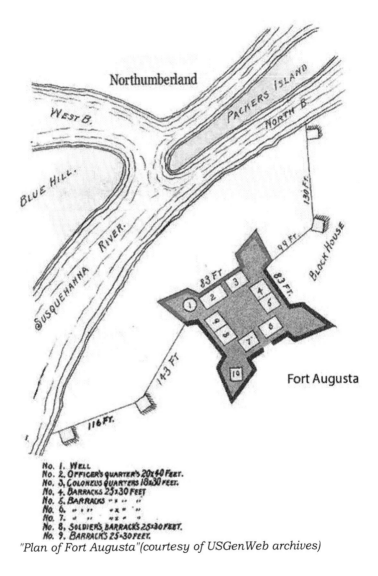

"Plan of Fort Augusta"(courtesy of USGenWeb archives)

The Belt had been an influential leader among Iroquois Indians living in the Ohio River Valley before the French military erected a chain of forts in the region during the early 1750s. He and a number of other Iroquois had moved to the Susquehanna after the English and French began fighting. In late 1755, these Indians were living at Harris's Ferry.

Harris mentioned this particular chief prominently in an October 20 letter to the governor:

"By report this evening I was ... informed by the Belt of Wampum and these Indians here there were seen near Shamokin, about six days ago, two French Indians of the Caughnawaga tribe. I a little doubted the truth of the report at first, but the Indians have seemed so afraid that they dispatched messengers immediately to the mountains above my house to bring in some of their women that were gathering chestnuts, for fear of their being killed."

Often referred to as "French Mohawks," the Caughnawaga lived at a French mission near Montreal. Caughnawaga warriors were frequently involved in raids either encouraged by or led by French soldiers.

Warfare had intensified along the Susquehanna by the end of October. "The Indians are cutting us off every day, and I had a certain account of about 1,500 Indians, besides French, being on their march against us and Virginia, and now close on our borders, their scouts scalping our families on our frontiers daily," Harris reported in an October 29 letter to the governor.

"Andrew Montour and others at Shamokin desired me to take care; that there was 40 Indians out many days and intended to burn my house and destroy myself and family," he added. "I have this day cut (loop)holes in my house, and am determined to hold out to the last extremity if I can get some men to stand by me."

In the event of an Indian attack, Harris intended to shoot his firearms through the loopholes.

The frontiersman also reported: "I have sent out two Indian spies to Shamokin. They are Mohawks, and I expect they will return in a day or two."

This move was more than warranted. "I am informed that a French officer was expected at Shamokin this week with a party of Delawares and Shawnees, no doubt to take possession of our river," Harris said.

Women Following Soldiers Irk Army Chaplain

July 1756

Establishing a fort along the Susquehanna River at present-day Sunbury was so important that Philadelphia-based Gov. Robert H. Morris traveled to Harris's Ferry (modern Harrisburg) to see Pennsylvania soldiers start their march upriver to build it.

The French & Indian War had begun in July 1755, and by May 1756, when the soldiers set out, Indians allied with the French were making continual attacks on Pennsylvania's northern and western frontiers. Morris saw the erection of Fort Augusta as a key countermeasure. For decades, the land at the Susquehanna confluence had been the site of a major Indian town called Shamokin.

The Iroquois had never formally sold the land at the forks to the Pennsylvania colony. Even so, the late Pennsylvania historian, William A. Hunter, said in "Forts on the Pennsylvania Frontier," that Gov. Morris "designated the site of present Sunbury, not only because this was the only land at the forks purchased from the Indians (privately, from Shikellamy) but also because 'the land on ye south side of the east branch ... opposite the middle of the island ... is the highest of any of the low land there about and the best place for a fort.'"

The marching orders of Col. William Clapham, who commanded the expedition, were clear:

"As to the place upon which this fort is to be erected, that must be in a great measure left to your judgment; but ... it must be on the east side of the Susquehanna; the lands on the west, at the forks, between the branches, not being purchased from the

Indians."

Clapham also took several cannons, and the governor said, "The guns you have with you will form a rampart of a moderate height, commanding the main river."

Pennsylvania's hastily organized military had already constructed a series of log forts at strategic spots along rivers and forest trails frequented by war parties. Fort Augusta would become the largest of these.

As the colonel proceeded upriver, in mid-June he encountered Ogaghradariha, an Iroquois who told him that he represented "the Iroquois living on the North Branch of Susquehanna" and that these Indians "agree to your building a fort at Shamokin."

In describing the colonel's conversations with this Indian, Hunter reported that the colonel asked Ogaghradariha to inform the Six Nations that he was about to build a fort at the Forks of the Susquehanna, and that "we hope they will not refuse us the liberty we now ask of building this fort." But Ogaghradariha later reported that he had been ill and thus hadn't been able to carry out Clapham's request.

Clapham's column consisted mainly of recruits. Few had prior military experience, and many of the four hundred soldiers had worked in the fur trade before the French & Indian War closed the frontier to commerce.

Before they marched, the soldiers built a fleet of twenty flat-bottom boats called batteaux to ship their supplies. A number of women also turned out to serve as cooks, nurses, and washerwomen.

The chaplain who accompanied the expedition was a middle-aged clergyman, the Rev. Charles Beatty. Entries from his journal offer colorful details of the expedition:

Monday, May 21: "Set off from Harris' ... Arrived safely at McKee's store (modern Dauphin), where we found the colonel.... Had but a poor night's lodging, not having my tent or any bedding."

Rev. Charles Beatty

Friday, June 4: "Major (James) Burd with the last division of the regiment joined us. Second Lt. George Allen and 40 men, dressed as Indians, sent out as scouts to Shamokin."

Saturday, June 5: "The colonel in the afternoon marched with four companies. Reached Foster's, about three miles, where we encamped."

Sunday, June 6: "Rose early; and after prayers, began our march; halted for breakfast after four miles, then marched on to Armstrong's (near present-day Halifax) when we encamped."

Monday, June 7: "Began to fell timber for building a fort 160 feet square, called Fort Halifax."

Tuesday, June 8: "Scouts returned, having gone only 18 miles when they imagined they were discovered and surrounded by the Indians. Many alarms, reports, and detentions."

Sabbath, June 13: "Received a proclamation from the governor of a cessation of arms against the Indians on the east side of the Susquehanna for 30 days, and at the same time an account of several persons killed and scalped at the forks of Swatara (north of present-day Lebanon) ..."

Saturday, June 19: "A number of the soldiers mutinied, chiefly Dutch."

Sabbath, June 20: "A general court-martial to try the prisoners, most of whom were discharged as innocent. This prevented most of the officers from attending (worship services). Preached upon conscience, with a particular application to those who mutinied."

Friday, June 21: "Ensign Atley came to camp, and brought up under guard two Dutchmen, deserters who had sacrilegiously mutilated an Indian in his grave."

Sabbath, June 27: "Were alarmed by the advance guard firing at a mark. The whole regiment were under arms, advanced immediately, expecting to engage every minute, which prevented sermon in the forenoon.

"So just as (worship) service began in the afternoon, (we) had another alarm, but few, alas! seemed to regret the disappointment (of canceling worship). Wickedness seems to increase in the camp, which gives me a great deal of uneasiness."

Wednesday, June 30: "Orders were given that all should march the next morning."

Thursday, July 1: "Up early to prepare for marching. Desired the colonel to leave the women behind, according to his promise, especially those of bad character.

"Accordingly they were all ordered to be paraded, and the major had orders to leave such as he saw fit behind; but when this came to be done, one of the officers pleaded for one, and another for another, saying that they could wash, etc., so that few were left of a bad character, and these would not stay but followed us that night, and kept with us."

Fort Halifax was twelve miles north of Fort Hunter. Had the colonel forced the women to return to the settlements, they would have had to walk through the forest for nearly a full day unarmed and without an escort.

Indian Fleet Descends River for Wintry Visit

March 1757

Winter made itself felt at Fort Augusta on Thursday, March 10, 1757. "This day it snowed so much that no work could be done," Major James Burd wrote in his journal.

Even so, soldiers keeping watch on the fort wall at noontime spotted a canoe coming down the Susquehanna River's North Branch with five Indians. They were flying the English flag, so that soldiers at the fort would know they were friendly and wouldn't shoot.

This occurred during the French and Indian War, and many Indians on the Pennsylvania frontier were siding with the French. The canoe landed, and Burd welcomed the travelers. They were Iroquois, and they showed the major that they carried a passport signed by William Denny, the governor of Pennsylvania.

"They ... told me they were ordered to inform me that ... 90 Indians more would be down here tomorrow or the next day," Burd wrote.

"I received the Indians kindly and told them I would receive them all in the same manner. They were pleased and thanked me," the major said.

The travelers asked Burd, who had become the fort's commandant earlier in the winter, to send the same message by an express to George Croghan, a frontiersman who was one of the colony's official Indian agents.

Croghan was often at Harris's Ferry (present-day Harrisburg), and "I accordingly sent John Lee, John Bonham, and Benjamin Nicholson off this night, 12 p.m., in a canoe," the major wrote.

Prepared from eyewitness observations in 1807, this engraving shows a river freighter passing through one of Schuyler's wing dams in the Mohawk while a large batteau waits its turn. (courtesy of the New York State Museum)

One of the Indians was a man named Nathaniel, and on the evening of Saturday, March 12, "Nathaniel informed me that he saw his brother at Tioga (present-day Athens on the North Branch), who told him he was just come from Fort DuQuesne (a French fort at modern Pittsburgh), and before he left that place that six Frenchmen and three Indians had set out from thence in order to come and view the works at Fort Augusta."

The largest of the Pennsylvania's frontier defenses, Fort Augusta was only nine months old. Colonial soldiers had begun to fortify the Susquehanna's confluence of the North and West branches in July 1756.

Although the fort's log walls were erected and several barracks had been constructed for the soldiers to live in, finishing work was still under way. For instance, Burd's March 9 journal entry noted that seventeen soldiers were cutting logs for the stockade wall surrounding the fort; thirty-seven men were setting these logs in the ground; and eight carpenters were cutting wood for a little house inside the walls.

Traveling during the winter often took longer than anticipated, and the other Indians required an extra day to reach Fort Augusta. At 2 p.m. on Sunday, March 13, "the Indian fleet (came) in sight with two stand of English colors flying, consisting of 15 canoes and three batteaux," the major wrote.

Batteaux were narrow, flat-bottom boats.

The Indians fired two rifles in a salute, "which I answered from the upper bastion of the pickets," Burd said.

There were nearly ninety Indians in the fleet —"many of which (were) kings and chiefs of their people"—and when they landed, Burd said he and his soldiers "welcomed them with three huzzahs," or cheers.

"They all expressed a good deal of satisfaction at their meeting us here and told me upon their arrival that they hurried to come here as they had good intelligence the French intended to besiege this fort, and they were afraid that the enemy would get (here) before them," Burd said in his journal.

That night, Burd and his officers met the Iroquois at a formal council in his house inside the fort. An Indian named Thomas was the Iroquois spokesman, and he presented three strings of wampum to the major.

"We are all one, we are brothers," Thomas declared. "The French have killed many of our people, but we all, the Six Nations, have counseled to be English from this time forth."

As time passed, Indians siding with the French occasionally ambushed patrols or work parties sent out into the countryside from the fort, but Fort Augusta itself was never attacked or besieged.

Hurt Bear Complicates Escape from Indians

March 1759

Soon after Indian warriors abducted Marie LeRoy and Barbara Leininger, teenage girls who had lived along Penns Creek in October 1755, the girls were forced to give up European-style clothing and to dress like Indians.

The Delaware Indian women responsible for them required them to wear dresses and moccasins made of deerskin and to wear their hair long. Not only were the girls discouraged from speaking their native languages —Barbara spoke German, and Marie, French—but they were also encouraged to learn the Delaware language. Within months after their capture, they were beginning to look more and more like Native Americans.

Marie and Barbara had been living in the Delaware town called Kittanning on the Allegheny River for at least eight months when Pennsylvania soldiers led by Lt. Col. John Armstrong attacked the town at daybreak in early September 1756.

The Indians had dogs, which started to bark as the soldiers rushed into the town and began shooting their rifles and muskets. Caught by surprise, the warriors grabbed their own weapons and began firing back. Soon some of the Indian houses had caught fire.

Kittanning occupied both sides of the Allegheny. The soldiers attacked the east side. Marie and Barbara lived across the river on the west side, where Indian women quickly rounded up as many captives as they could and took them into the forest away from the town.

"We were immediately conveyed 10 miles farther into the interior in order that we might have no chance of trying ... to escape," the girls said afterwards.

There were dozens of white captives living in the town, but the Pennsylvania soldiers managed to liberate only ten or twelve of them. The girls from Penns Creek weren't among them. When they returned to Kittanning, they saw that many of the wigwams and cabins on the east shore had burned to the ground.

Soon after that, many Kittanning Indians moved farther west to get beyond the reach of the Pennsylvanians.

Two years later, Barbara and Marie were still living as Indian captives. Their village was in eastern Ohio, about one hundred miles west of the newly settled Pittsburgh. The girls were about eighteen, and the Indian women had decided that Marie should get married. Marie was distraught to learn they had even picked out an Indian man for her. She told a friend that "she would sooner be shot than have him for her husband."

This friend was Owen Gibson, a young man who had lived in what is now Perry County before Indians captured him near Robison's Fort along Sherman Creek in July 1756. Marie confided that she and Barbara were planning to escape and persuaded Gibson to join them.

Anyone meeting Gibson would have easily mistaken him for a young Indian man, because he wore his hair Indian-style and dressed in a loin cloth, leggings, and moccasins. A Delaware leader, Pisquetomen, regarded Gibson as his adopted brother and allowed him to have firearms for hunting. As a result, Gibson had become a skilled hunter during his captivity.

The fourth prisoner who joined the conspiracy was David Breckenridge, a young man who had been a wagon driver at the time of his capture.

The four sneaked away from the village after dark on March 16, 1759. "We had to pass many huts ... and knew that there were at least 16 dogs with them.... Not a single one of these dogs barked," the girls said later.

The village sat on the bank of the Muskingum River. When the runaways came to a raft belonging to an Indian, "we got on board and pushed off. But we were carried almost a mile down the river before we could reach the other side. There our journey began in good earnest," the girls said. "Full of anxiety and fear, we fairly ran that whole night and all the next day, when we lay down to rest without venturing to kindle a fire."

Their flight through the forest to the new British fort at present-day Pittsburgh was dangerous. One morning, for instance, "Owen Gibson fired at a bear. The animal fell, but when he ran with his tomahawk to kill it, it jumped up and bit him in the feet, leaving three wounds. We all hastened to his assistance. The bear escaped," the girls said.

It took the runaways two weeks to reach Fort Pitt. Late in the afternoon of March 31, they stood on the bank of the Monongahela River and shouted across to the fort. An officer sent soldiers in a rowboat to determine the reason for the shouting. In the twilight, the soldiers were wary about getting too close to the shore. The teenagers looked like Indians, not colonists, and the soldiers feared they were being lured into a trap.

As Marie and Barbara said later: "They thought we were Indians, and wanted us to spend the night where we were, saying they would fetch us in the morning. When we had succeeded in convincing them that we were English prisoners who had escaped from the Indians and that we were wet and cold and hungry, they brought us over."

Their days as Indian captives had ended. At the fort Colonel Hugh Mercer "helped and aided us in every way which lay in his power ... (and) ordered for each of us a new chemise, a petticoat, a pair of stockings, garters, and a knife," the girls said.

Hugh Mercer

Attack Threat Prompts West Branch Settlers to Flee

July 1778

When the Rev. Philip Vickers Fithian traveled through Northumberland in June 1775, he saw much activity on the Susquehanna River.

"Here are a number of boatmen employed in going up and down the river to Middletown and back," the clergyman noted in his diary. "With these and others from the country, this infant village seems busy and noisy as a Philadelphia ferry house."

There was good reason for this. As settlers of European descent moved into the Susquehanna Valley during the 1760s and 1770s, they established farms high up both the West and North branches.

As Fithian observed while riding along the West Branch, "The road lies along the river, and after leaving the town a mile, such a fertile, level, goodly country I have perhaps never seen—wheat and rye, thick and very high. Oats I saw in many places ..."

When farmers began producing abundant quantities of wheat, rye, and other crops, enterprising boatmen started shipping their surplus farm goods down the Susquehanna to Middletown, about sixty-five miles south of Sunbury.

Middletown, which occupied the spot where Swatara Creek emptied into the Susquehanna, had become a river port where upriver commodities were transferred from boats to horse-drawn wagons, which teamsters hauled over dirt roads to markets in Lancaster and Philadelphia.

The American Revolution had begun by the time of Fithian's visit, a fact that colored his July 2 description of a visit to the home of William Scull, a Northumberland surveyor.

"While we were at coffee, the post came into town," Fithian wrote. "We have in the papers accounts of the battle at Bunker's Hill, near Boston ... (and) accounts of General Washington and his aid-de-camp, Mr. Mifflin, leaving Philadelphia for the North American camp."

By early 1778, the war had come much closer to the valley. Hostile Indians accompanied by Tories and British soldiers occasionally raided the valley, and this was worrisome to Col. Samuel Hunter, the commandant at Fort Augusta, which sat on the riverbank at Sunbury and overlooked the Susquehanna's confluence.

Hunter was responsible for protecting a large section of Central Pennsylvania, and his correspondence shows that he saw a strong need to fortify the widespread settlements.

On May 14, for example, Hunter wrote, "I have ordered some people that lives nigh (near) the Great Island (across from Lock Haven) to preserve shad and barrel them up for the use of the militia that will be stationed there this summer.... We are scarce of guns, not more than one half of the militia is provided with arms, and a number of them very ordinary. Our powder is exceeding bad, and not fit for rifles in any shape. And as for flints we can get none to buy ..."

As ill-equipped as Hunter's soldiers were, the settlers felt especially vulnerable when in early July, there were signs of hostile Indians in the West Branch Valley. Then came news that British rangers and their Indian allies had massacred the soldiers defending the Connecticut settlements in the Wyoming Valley along the North Branch. Along both branches, hundreds of settlers fled from their homes and headed for the protection of Fort Augusta.

As scout Robert Covenhoven reported afterwards of his trip up and down the West Branch:

"I took my family safely to Sunbury, and came back in a keel-boat to secure my furniture. Just as I rounded a point above Derrstown, (present-day Lewisburg), I met a whole convoy from all the forts above. Such a sight I never saw in my life. Boats, canoes, hog troughs, rafts hastily made of dry sticks, every sort of floating article had been put in requisition and were crowded with women, children, and plunder. Whenever an obstruction occurred at any shoal or ripple, the women would leap out into the water and put their shoulders to the boat or raft and launch it again into deep water. The men of the settlement came down in single file, on each side of the river, to guard women and children."

To everyone's relief, no hostiles appeared, and the West Branch refugees made it safely to Fort Augusta.

Cattle Starved During March to Fort Augusta

May 1779

During the summer of 1779, red tape did as much as low water to slow the shipment of military supplies up the Susquehanna River from Harris's Ferry, first to Sunbury and then on to Wilkes-Barre where American soldiers were preparing to march into the Finger Lakes Region.

The Revolutionary War was well under way, and Gen. George Washington had ordered Maj. Gen. John Sullivan to invade Iroquois country in what is now western New York State. To do this, Sullivan gathered an army of several thousand soldiers along the river in the Wyoming Valley. Before he could start, his men had to have provisions.

Most supplies for the expedition were to come up the Susquehanna in flat-bottom boats, but wagons were also essential, if only to move provisions overland from mills and farms to the docks where boats awaited them.

Col. Thomas Hartley underscored this in a May 11, 1779, letter to Joseph Reed, president of Pennsylvania's Executive Council. The York County commissary had procured ample of provisions, but lacked transportation to ship them to the river, Hartley said, writing from York.

"Unfortunately, no wagons can be provided in the ordinary course to transport the flour to Harris's Ferry (present-day Harrisburg), where the boats are to receive the same," Hartley declared. "The unhappy situation of the frontiers requires every exertion. The river is getting low.... The distance is not thirty miles from York."

Maj. Gen. John Sullivan

Hartley's persuasive prose got the wagons moving. The wagons were pressed into service, and the flour got shipped upriver.

By mid-summer Sullivan found himself under fire from critics for taking too long to march into enemy territory. On July 31 the general reported that the army's suppliers had sent spoiled food to his soldiers. "The inspector is now on the ground ... inspecting the provisions, and his regard to the truth must oblige him on his return to report that of the salted meat on hand, there is not a single pound fit to be eaten ..."

There was another difficulty. Suppliers were driving livestock upriver from the agricultural regions of Pennsylvania even though the forested country along the river north of Harrisburg lacked suitable pasture for them. Consequently, the cows couldn't find adequate food.

"About 150 cattle sent to Sunbury were left there, being too poor to walk, and many of them unable to stand," Sullivan said.

Despite the many difficulties confronting Sullivan, hundreds of soldiers and boatmen spent at least part of the summer of '79 toiling on the Susquehanna and shipping supplies to Sullivan's army. One of them was 1st Lt. John Hardenbergh of the Second New York Continental Regiment.

Hardenbergh's journal includes a detailed sketch of his nine-day, 130-mile roundtrip from the army camp near Wilkes-Barre down to Sunbury for provisions. Old-growth forest came down to river's edge along much of the way. Midway stood Fort Jenkins, a stockade post on the riverbank.

In Hardenbergh's words:

Sunday, June 20: "I was ordered to go down the River Susquehanna with a party in boats under the command of Captain (Charles) Graham. Left Wyoming about 7 o'clock in the morning and arrived with the boats at Fort Jenkins at sunset and stayed that night."

This fort had a garrison of about one hundred men and was located just south of the spot where Interstate 80 now crosses the North Branch between Berwick and Bloomsburg.

June 21: "Left Fort Jenkins in the morning, proceeded down the river and arrived at Northumberland town, dined there, and proceeded to Sunbury and arrived there at 7 o'clock at night."

Overlooking the river at Sunbury stood Fort Augusta, an old French & Indian War post.

Pennsylvania had refortified the 1756 structure when the Revolution brought new waves of Indian raids against the white settlements along the West and North Branches.

June 22: "Laid still at Sunbury and loaded the boats with flour and beef."

June 23: "At 9 o'clock in the morning left Sunbury, proceeded up the river about eight miles."

June 24: "Proceeded up the river till night and lodged on board the boat. In the night lost my hat."

June 25: "Proceeded up the river as far as Fort Jenkins and lodged there."

June 26: "Left Fort Jenkins and arrived at the falls. Got half the boats up the falls, which were drawn up by ropes."

These falls, located near present-day Berwick, were more like rapids than a cascade over a waterfall.

June 27: "Got up the rest of the boats, and proceeded up the river and halted along shore overnight. Col. (Mattias) Ogden's regiment from Jersey was sent down as a guard to us from Wyoming."

June 28: "At reveille beat proceeded up the river to the upper falls. Got all the boats up, (one of which overset in going up) and arrived at Shawnee flats about four miles from Wyoming."

June 29: "Left Shawnee flats in the morning and arrived at Wyoming about 7 o'clock in the morning, unloaded the boats and went up to camp in the afternoon to Jacob's Plains."

Now part of Plains Township, Jacob's Plains was along the North Branch just north of Wilkes-Barre.

Skeleton, Skulls Visible on Battlefield Visit

July 1779

July 2, 1779: A handful of horsemen, all officers in George Washington's Continental Army, slowly ride through the trees and tall grass covering a year-old battlefield along the Susquehanna River's North Branch.

Their eyes scour the ground as they look for the bones of Connecticut soldiers killed in the Wyoming Valley a year earlier. Suddenly one of the riders spots the remains of a man still wearing a coat, and everybody dismounts for a closer look.

"A captain's commission with 17 continental dollars was found in the pocket of the skeleton of a man, who had laid above ground 12 months," reports Major James Norris of the 3rd New Hampshire Regiment.

Norris and the other horsemen were officers in the 1779 expedition that Maj. Gen. John Sullivan organized to go into western New York State. The Revolutionary War was in its fifth year, and General Washington wanted Sullivan to bring about "the total destruction and devastation" of the settlements of Iroquois Indians allied with the British. Sullivan's soldiers were to burn their towns, "ruin their crops now in the ground and prevent their planting more."

A year earlier—on July 3, 1778—an army of Tories and Indians had invaded the Wyoming Valley and defeated the settlers who turned out to repel the invasion. They killed about three hundred of the valley's defenders—mostly men from Connecticut who had settled in the valley—and then looted and burned

Wyoming Valley Massacre

houses, barns, and other places that hadn't been directly affected by the fighting.

The Wyoming settlements were officially part of Connecticut, and many men from the Wyoming Valley had been away, serving in Connecticut regiments in Washington's army.

The next summer Sullivan gathered his army in the vicinity of Wilkes-Barre and waited for flat-bottom boats from Fort Augusta at Sunbury to come up the Susquehanna with provisions for the long march into Iroquois country.

Major Norris arrived at Wilkes-Barre on June 23, 1779, with the 3rd New Hampshire Regiment, which came up a new road cut through the forests from Easton. As Norris noted in his journal:

"About 12 o'clock we entered the town of Wyoming, which exhibits a melancholy scene of desolation, in ruined houses, wasted fields and fatherless children and widows.... Their houses were plundered and burnt, their cattle and effects conveyed away after they had capitulated; and the poor, helpless women and children obliged to skulk in the mountains and perish or travel down to the inhabitants, hungry, naked, and unsupported."

On June 27 the New Hampshire soldiers "were ordered to move off their ground and pitch (their tents) upon the Plains of Abraham, three miles higher up on the western bank of the Susquehanna ... The place of our camp (is) near an old stockade fort built by the inhabitants and called Forty Fort from 40 persons to whom the grant of the Wyoming lands was made by the government of Connecticut."

Norris and the other officers toured the battleground as the first anniversary of the Wyoming Massacre approached.

"We saw a stockade fort with a covert way to a fountain, which our guide told us was built for a show by some of the disaffected inhabitants and given up to the enemy immediately upon their approach.

"We examined the trees where the line of battle was formed, but found very few marks of an obstinate engagement: it appears indeed that the enemy were superior in numbers to the militia and soon after the commencement of the action turned their left flank. This brought on a retreat, in which the savages massacred upwards of two hundred men.

"We saw ... bones scattered over the ground for near two miles, and several skulls brought in at different times that had been scalped and inhumanly mangled with the hatchet."

Norris had more to report:

"Our guide showed us where 73 bodies had been buried in one hole.... All the houses along this river have been burnt; and the gardens and fields—the most fertile I ever beheld—grown over with weeds and bushes."

After the victorious Tories and Indians left, most of the surviving settlers fled. Many went down the North Branch and sought refuge at Fort Augusta. Others returned to Connecticut. The major's journal makes it plain that they were in such a hurry they didn't take the time to bury all of the men killed in the battle.

Among the survivors was Col. Zebulon Butler, who had commanded the Wyoming men. He was still living along the Susquehanna the next summer, and Major Norris described Butler's visit to the New Hampshire troops on July 13:

"Col. Butler showed us a death mall, or war mallet, that the Indians left by a man they had knocked on the head. The handle resembles that of a hatchet.... It is made of the root of a tree with a large ball worked on the head of it, and looks not much unlike a four-pound shot (cannonball) in the bill of an eagle, with a tuft of feathers on the crown. The end of the handle shows the face of a wildcat."

Delawares Trapping Beavers in the Rockies

September 1836

Born in Maine in 1814, Osborne Russell was that rarity among the Rocky Mountain trappers during the 1830s: a journalist with a keen eye for detail and a droll sense of humor.

Competition among trappers was fierce. "It was not a good policy for a trapper to let too many know where he intends to set his traps, particularly if his horse is not so fast as those of his companions," Russell wrote.

During the winters, when the snow was too deep for hunting and trapping, Russell read the poetry of Shakespeare and Byron. The journal he kept during his eight years (1834-1842) in the Rockies described several friendly encounters with Delaware Indians who, like Russell, were out trapping beavers for the fur trade.

These Delawares were the descendants of the Delaware Indians who had lived in Pennsylvania during the late 1600s and first half of the 1700s. By 1760, nearly all had left the colony. Some had moved north, and others, west.

Russell and his comrades were frequently members of a brigade led by Jim Bridger of the Rocky Mountain Fur Co. Often they had to contend with Blackfoot Indians, who, as Russell's journal entries show, were hostile to whites as well as other Indians.

Sept. 1, 1836: "We returned to the camp ... where we found ... 10 Delaware Indians who had joined the camp in order to hunt beaver with greater security."

Sept. 2: "Traveled down the Yellowstone River about 20 miles. This is a beautiful country, the large plains widely extending on either side of the river, intersected with streams and occasional low spurs of mountains.... Thousands of buffaloes may be seen in almost every direction, and deer, elk, and grizzly bear are abundant."

Sept. 7: The trappers had moved their camp to a tributary of the Yellowstone. "When we arrived at camp, we were told the sad news of the death of a French trapper named Bodah, who had been waylaid and killed by a party of Blackfeet.... One of the Delawares had been shot through the hip by the rifle of one of his comrades going off accidentally, and several war parties of Blackfeet had been seen scouting the country."

Sept. 9: "Blackfeet warriors surprised two men belonging to Russell's group as they were setting traps along the tributary. As the trappers ran off, the Indians shot one through the chest. His name was Howell, and he eventually died of the wound.

"About an hour after he was brought in, 20 whites and Delawares went to scour the brush along the river and fight the Blackfeet. Having found them, they drove them onto an island and fought them until dark."

One of the trappers, a Nez Perce Indian, was killed, "and one white slightly wounded in the shoulder," Russell reported. "The Blackfeet ... drew off in the night, secreting their dead and carrying off their wounded."

The trappers spent the winter of 1836-37 at a camp along the Yellowstone. In late February 1837, they broke camp and rode east to the Big Horn River where they set up camp. There were many Blackfeet Indians in the region, so Jim Bridger had the men fortify their camp by building breastworks of logs and brush.

March 25: "About sunrise, one solitary savage (a Blackfoot) crept up between the trees and shot about 200 yards at Mr. Bridger's cook as he was gathering wood outside the fort."

Jim Bridger

The trappers started out on their spring hunt on April 1 and headed west along a tributary of the Big Horn.

April 4: "After we had encamped, four Delawares who were cruising about in the hills hunting buffalo fell in with a party of 10 or 12 Blackfeet, killed one on the spot, and wounded several more. The Blackfeet then took to their heels and left the victorious Delawares without loss except one horse being slightly wounded in the neck."

While working along the Madison River in Wyoming and Montana in June 1838, Russell and his colleagues found themselves in a gun fight with Blackfeet. One of Russell's group was "an old Iroquois trapper ... (who) stripped himself entirely naked, throwing his powder horn and bullet pouch over his shoulder and taking his rifle in hand, began to dance and utter the shrill war cry of his nation. Twenty of us who stood around and near him cheered ... He started and we followed," Russell reported.

The fighting didn't last long. "Although seven or eight times our number, they retreated from rock to rock like hunted rats ...," Russell reported.

Two Thousand-mile Trip on Roads, Canals Cost $387

September 1839

In early September 1839, family matters propelled Hannah Bennett, a Wilkes-Barre woman, to go to Indiana. She traveled by stagecoach, railroad, river boat, and canal barge. She also kept a diary, which survives.

Her father, Joseph Slocum, and sister, Harriet Slocum, also went, and the three often changed their mode of transportation. At Montrose, for instance, they took a four-horse stagecoach to Binghamton, N.Y.

South of Ithaca, they took a train that used horses, not locomotives, to pull the cars.

Hannah noted: "We took our seats in what ought to have been a comfortable railroad car, but proved to be an old worn-out stage body, loaded with passengers and baggage.... The horses were lame and broken down."

At Ithaca "we went on board the steamboat DeWitt Clinton. The name is worthy of a better boat; she tows many freight boats; therefore, her progress is slow."

At Rochester they bought tickets on a packet boat that traveled through the night along the Erie Canal.

"Our boat was crowded," Hannah wrote. It left Rochester, headed west, at 10 p.m., and passengers slept in beds arranged in tiers, bunk-bed fashion.

"There was an attempt in the night, by one of the passengers, to rob Father," Hannah said. The man "lodged under him, and he put his hand in his pocket, which awakened Father, and therefore he did not succeed."

On September 28 the travelers reached Peru, Ind., about six hundred miles west of Wilkes-Barre. The trip had taken nineteen days.

The sisters and their father had a special reason for making such a long and, for the times at least, expensive journey. They had gone to visit their father's sister, Frances Slocum. As a five-year-old child, Frances had been kidnapped in 1778 by Delaware Indians from her home in Wilkes-Barre, then a frontier village. In 1837 Joseph and two of his siblings had found Frances, now a sixty-four-year-old grandmother, living among the Miami Indians near Peru. Two years later, Joseph took Hannah and Harriet to Indiana to meet the long-lost aunt, who for all practical purposes had become an Indian and who no longer spoke any English.

The visit lasted several days, but by October 3, the Pennsylvanians were headed home. The Indianapolis stagecoach went through a dense forest. "For want of stones and earth, they are under the necessity of making their roads and bridges of split timber and poles, which makes traveling rough and unpleasant," Hannah wrote.

At Cincinnati, they boarded a steamboat, the Royal, that headed up the Ohio River. The river was low, and "we ran aground several times." When the boat hit a sand bar "from which they could not extricate us," Hannah and her companions boarded a smaller boat that was having more success in avoiding sandbars. When the captain encountered low water, he made male passengers walk along the riverbank.

"We were much frightened," Hannah said.

At Wheeling, W.Va., "the boat struck a rock and stove a hole in her bottom. The captain turned her towards shore, ordered her fires out, and she soon filled with water." The passengers were evacuated, and, once ashore, found overnight accommodations.

In the morning Hannah's party hired a horse-drawn carriage and set out. When Hannah realized she

Steamboats in Cincinnati before the Civil War.

had left "my traveling bag" at Wheeling, "I wrote a note back and received it the next day."

At Pittsburgh—"a rich manufacturing town, but not pleasant to live in on account of the dense smoke"—the travelers took a canal boat bound for the Susquehanna River. West of Johnstown, the packet passed through a nine hundred-foot-long tunnel. They ate breakfast as they ascended the Allegheny Mountain on the portage railroad. At Hollidaysburg they boarded "the Juniata packet, which started immediately for Harrisburg. In 38 miles, there were 53 locks, which makes slow traveling."

It was late Saturday when the boat neared the Susquehanna canal, and Captain Vogelsong, fearing his passengers might miss their connection, "ran a mile to hail the Susquehanna boat that we might not be detained over Sunday."

"The boat in which we came to Northumberland went up the West Branch," so they changed to a North

Branch boat. They "stopped a few minutes at Danville" where they "saw Mr. and Mrs. Shoales."

They reached Wilkes-Barre on October 28. They had been on the road six weeks and six days, and had traveled about two thousand miles.

"It cost us $387.69," Hannah reported.

Selected Bibliography

Hunter, William A. "Forts of the Pennsylvania Frontier, 1753-1758." Harrisburg: Pennsylvania Historical and Museum Commission, 1960.

Pennsylvania Archives, First Series. Vols. I and II. Edited by Samuel Hazard. Philadelphia: Joseph Severns & Co., 1853.

Heckewelder, John Gottlieb Ernestus. "An Account of the History, Manners, and Customs of the Indian Nations, Who Once Inhabited Pennsylvania and the Neighboring States." Philadelphia: Publication Fund of the Historical Society of Pennsylvania, 1876. (Reprint edition by Arno Press Inc., 1971)

Hsiung, David C. "Death on the Juniata: Delawares, Iroquois, and Pennsylvanians in a Colonial Whodunit" Pennsylvania History: A Journal of Mid-Atlantic Studies (Vol. 64, No. 4) Autumn 1998.

Meginness, John F. "Biography of Frances Slocum, The Lost Sister of Wyoming." Williamsport, Pa.: Heller Bros. Printing House, 1891.

Rupp, I. Daniel. "History and Topography of Dauphin, Cumberland, Franklin, Bedford, Adams and Perry Counties." Lancaster: Gilbert Hills, Proprietor & Publisher, 1846.

Swift, Robert B. "The Mid-Appalachian Frontier: A Guide to Historic Sites of the French and Indian War." Gettysburg, Pa.: Thomas Publications, 2001.

Wallace, Paul A.W. "Indians in Pennsylvania." Harrisburg: Pennsylvania Historical and Museum Commission, 1970.

Wallace, Paul A.W. "Indian Paths of Pennsylvania." Harrisburg: Pennsylvania Historical and Museum Commission, 1971.

52935809R00061

Made in the USA
San Bernardino, CA
01 September 2017